A Very Merry QUILTED CHRISTMAS™

2

22

DESIGN BY WENDY SHEPPARD
QUILTED BY DARLENE SZABO OF SEW GRACEFUL QUILTING

Christmas Is Fir Real

Juxtaposing light and dark fabrics gives a 3-D effect to the trees!

SKILL LEVEL
Confident Beginner

FINISHED SIZES
Quilt Size: 49" x 60"
Block Size: 8" x 12"
Number of Blocks: 20

MATERIALS
- 3¼ yards cream tonal*
- ¾ yard each light green, light red, dark green and dark red prints*
- ½ yard each turquoise and binding prints*
- ⅛ yard burgundy print*
- 3½ yards backing*
- 57" x 68" batting*
- Thread*
- Basic sewing tools and supplies

Fabrics from the Cozy Wonderland collection by Stephanie Sliwinski of Fancy That Design House for Moda Fabrics; 50 wt. thread from Aurifil; and Tuscany Silk batting from Hobbs Bonded Fibers used to make sample. EQ8 was used to design this quilt.

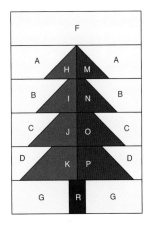

Short Tree
8" x 12" Finished Block
Make 10

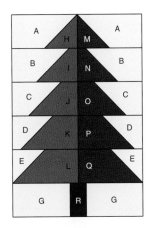

Tall Tree
8" x 12" Finished Block
Make 10

PROJECT NOTES

Read all instructions before beginning this project.

Stitch right sides together using a ¼" seam allowance unless otherwise specified.

Materials and cutting lists assume 40" of usable fabric width for yardage.

Arrows indicate directions to press seams.

WOF – width of fabric

HST – half-square triangle

QST – quarter-square triangle

CUTTING

From length of cream tonal cut:

- 4 (4" x 42") G strips
- 2 (3" x 55½") V border strips
- 2 (3" x 49½") W border strips
- 3 (1½" x 44½") T strips
- 10 (2½" x 8½") F rectangles
- 40 (2½" x 4½") A rectangles
- 40 (2½" x 4") B rectangles
- 40 (2½" x 3½") C rectangles
- 40 (2½" x 3") D rectangles
- 20 (2½") E squares
- 16 (1½" x 12½") S rectangles

From each light green and light red print cut:

- 10 (2½" x 4") K rectangles (20 total)
- 10 (2½" x 3½") J rectangles (20 total)
- 10 (2½" x 3") I rectangles (20 total)
- 10 (2½") H squares (20 total)

From remaining light red print cut:

- 10 (2½" x 4½") L rectangles

From each dark green and dark red print cut:

- 10 (2½" x 4") P rectangles (20 total)
- 10 (2½" x 3½") O rectangles (20 total)
- 10 (2½" x 3") N rectangles (20 total)
- 10 (2½") M squares (20 total)

From remaining dark red print cut:

- 10 (2½" x 4½") Q rectangles

From turquoise print cut:

- 5 (1½" x WOF) strips; stitch short ends to short ends, then subcut into:
    4 (1½" x 44½") U strips

From burgundy print cut:

- 2 (1½" x WOF) R strips

From binding fabric cut:

- 6 (2½" x WOF) binding strips

COMPLETING THE BLOCKS

1. Refer to Sew & Flip Corners on page 11 to add a corner triangle on the lower right corner of one A rectangle using an H square to complete one A-H unit (Figure 1). Make 20.

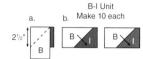

A-H Unit
Make 10 each

Figure 1

2. Position a B rectangle perpendicular on the left end of one I rectangle. Measure and mark a dot 2½" down from the top left corner of B, then draw a diagonal line from the upper right corner of B to the dot (Figure 2a). Sew on the drawn line, then trim the seam to ¼" to complete one B-I unit (Figure 2b). Make 20.

B-I Unit
Make 10 each

Figure 2

3. Repeat step 2 to make 20 C-J units using 20 each C and J rectangles (Figure 3a) and 20 D-K units using 20 each D and K rectangles (Figure 3b). Then make 10 E-L units using 10 each E squares and L rectangles (Figure 3c).

C-J Units
Make 10 each

D-K Units
Make 10 each

E-L Unit
Make 10

Figure 3

4. Refer again to Sew & Flip Corners to add a corner triangle on the lower left corner of one A rectangle using an M square to complete one A-M unit (Figure 4). Make 20.

A-M Unit
Make 10 each

Figure 4

5. Position a B rectangle perpendicular on the right end of one N rectangle. Measure and mark a dot 2½" down from the top right corner of B, then draw a diagonal line from the upper left corner of B to the dot (Figure 5a). Sew on the drawn line, then trim the seam to ¼" to complete one B-N unit (Figure 5b). Make 20.

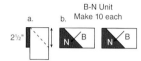

B-N Unit
Make 10 each

Figure 5

6. Repeat step 5 to make 20 C-O units using 20 each C and O rectangles (Figure 6a) and 20 D-P units using 20 each D and P rectangles (Figure 6b). Then make 10 E-Q units using 10 each E squares and Q rectangles (Figure 6c).

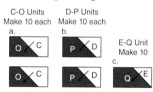

C-O Units
Make 10 each

D-P Units
Make 10 each

E-Q Unit
Make 10

Figure 6

7. Sew one G strip to each long side of an R strip to make a strip set. Make two strip sets. Cut 20 (2½" x 8½") G-R-G units from the strip sets (Figure 7).

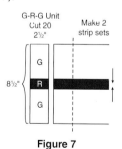

G-R-G Unit
Cut 20
2½"

Make 2 strip sets

8½"

Figure 7

8. To make one Tall Tree block, gather one each matching E-L, D-K, C-J, B-I and A-H unit. Also gather one each matching E-Q, D-P, C-O, B-N and A-M unit. Arrange the units in two columns; sew into columns, then sew the columns together. Sew a G-R-G unit to the bottom to complete one Tall Tree block (Figure 8). Make 10.

Make 10

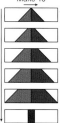

Figure 8

9. To make one Short Tree block, gather one each matching D-K, C-J, B-I and A-H unit. Also gather one each matching D-P, C-O, B-N and A-M unit. Arrange the units in two columns; sew into columns, then sew the columns together. Sew one F rectangle to the top and a G-R-G unit to the bottom to complete one Short Tree block (Figure 9). Make 10.

Make 10

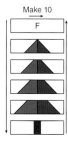

Figure 9

COMPLETING THE QUILT

1. Referring to the Assembly Diagram, arrange the Tall Tree blocks, Short Tree blocks, and S, T and U strips in 11 rows. Sew into rows, then sew the rows together to complete the quilt center.

2. Sew the V border strips to the sides of the quilt center and the W border strips to the top and bottom to complete the quilt top.

3. Layer, baste, quilt as desired and bind referring to Quilting Basics. The photographed quilt was quilted with an allover swirly design. ●

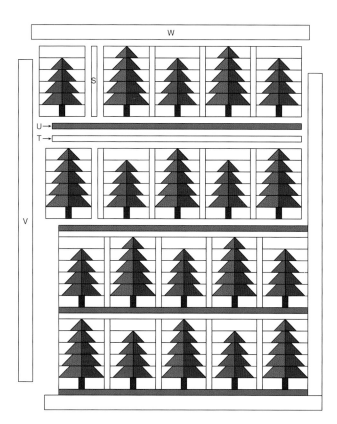

Christmas Is Fir Real
Assembly Diagram 49" x 60"

DESIGN BY LYN BROWN
QUILTED BY CINDY KRUSE

Noel Surrounded

Update the traditional Burgoyne Surrounded block for Christmas. Just six large blocks bring a modern vibe to this age-old design.

SKILL LEVEL
Confident Beginner

FINISHED SIZES
Quilt Size: 54" x 76½"
Block Size: 22½" x 22½"
Number of Blocks: 6

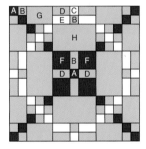

Burgoyne Surrounded
22½" x 22½" Finished Block
Make 6

MATERIALS
- 5¼ yards green tonal*
- 1 yard each red tonal and white solid*
- ¾ yard red stripe*
- 4¾ yards backing*
- 63" x 85" batting
- Thread
- Basic sewing tools and supplies

Fabrics from Hoffman California-International Fabrics used to make sample.

PROJECT NOTES
Read all instructions before beginning this project.

Stitch right sides together using a ¼" seam allowance unless otherwise specified.

Materials and cutting lists assume 40" of usable fabric width for yardage.

Arrows indicate directions to press seams.

WOF – width of fabric
HST – half-square triangle
QST – quarter-square triangle

CUTTING:

From length of green tonal cut:
- 2 (5" x 68") K border strips
- 2 (5" x 45½") L border strips
- 6 (3½" x 42") D strips
- 14 (2" x 42") B strips
- 24 (5" x 8") H rectangles
- 48 (3½" x 5") G rectangles
- 8 (2" x 3½") I rectangles

From red tonal cut:
- 4 (3½" x WOF) F strips
- 7 (2" x WOF) A strips
- 4 (2") J squares

"During the American Revolution, the colonial forces met the British in battle at Saratoga. The British general was 'Gentleman Johnny' Burgoyne and his 7,000 men far outnumbered the Americans. However, by loosely surrounding the large British force with smaller bands of colonists, the colonists prevailed. This block pattern illustrates that battle, with Burgoyne's large force in the center of the block and the smaller groups of Americans surrounding them. The Battle of Saratoga was a turning point in the American War for Independence."
—Lyn Brown

From white solid cut:
- 4 (3½" x WOF) E strips
- 7 (2" x WOF) C strips

From red stripe cut:
- 7 (2½" x WOF) binding strips

Here's a Tip

Don't be intimidated by the many pieces in this block. Individual units are easily made using strip piecing methods. Block assembly is a snap with whole cloth rectangles connecting the units.

COMPLETING THE BLOCKS

Note: *Pay close attention to fabric orientation in all steps.*

1. Sew one each A and B strip together lengthwise to make a strip set. Make three strip sets. Cut 56 (2" x 3½") A-B units from strip sets (Figure 1).

Figure 1

2. Sew two A-B units together to complete one four-patch unit (Figure 2). Make 28. Set aside 4 for border assembly.

Four-Patch Unit
Make 28

Figure 2

3. Sew one A strip to one long edge of a B strip, then sew a C strip to the opposite edge to make a strip set. Make three strip sets. Cut 48 (2" x 5") A-B-C units from the strip sets (Figure 3).

Figure 3

4. Sew one B strip to each long edge of a C strip to make a strip set. Make two strip sets. Cut 24 (2" x 5") B-C-B units from the strip sets (Figure 4).

Figure 4

5. Arrange two A-B-C units and one B-C-B unit in three rows; sew together to complete one nine-patch unit (Figure 5). Make 24.

Nine-Patch Unit
Make 24

Figure 5

6. Sew one D strip to each long edge of a C strip to make a strip set. Make two strip sets. Cut 24 (2" x 8") D-C-D units from the strip sets (Figure 6).

Figure 6

7. Sew one E strip to each long edge of a B strip to make a strip set. Make two strip sets. Cut 24 (2" x 8") E-B-E units from the strip sets (Figure 7).

Figure 7

8. Sew one D-C-D unit to the top of one E-B-E unit to complete one six-patch unit (Figure 8). Make 24.

Six-Patch Unit
Make 24

Figure 8

9. Sew one F strip to each long edge of a B strip to make a strip set. Make two strip sets. Cut 12 (3½" x 8") F-B-F units from the strip sets (Figure 9).

Figure 9

10. Sew one D strip to each long edge of an A strip to make a strip set. Cut six (2" x 8") D-A-D units from the strip set (Figure 10).

Figure 10

11. Arrange two F-B-F units and one D-A-D unit in three rows; sew together to complete one center unit (Figure 11). Make six.

Center Unit
Make 6

Figure 11

12. Arrange one center unit, eight G rectangles and four each four-patch units, nine-patch units, six-patch units and H rectangles in five rows; sew into rows, then sew the rows together to complete one Burgoyne Surrounded block (Figure 12). Make six.

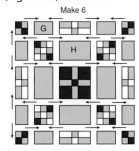

Figure 12

COMPLETING THE TOP/BOTTOM BORDERS

1. Gather the four-patch units that were set aside in step 2 of Completing the Blocks. Arrange one four-patch unit, two I rectangles and one J square in two rows; sew into rows, then sew the rows together to complete one corner unit (Figure 13). Make four.

Corner Unit
Make 4

Figure 13

2. Sew a corner unit to each end of one L strip to complete one top/bottom border (Figure 14). Make two.

Top/Bottom Border
Make 2

Figure 14

COMPLETING THE QUILT

1. Referring to the Assembly Diagram, arrange the Burgoyne Surrounded blocks in three rows; sew into rows, then sew the rows together to complete the quilt center.

2. Sew the K border strips to the sides of the quilt center and the top/bottom borders to the top and bottom to complete the quilt top.

3. Layer, baste, quilt as desired and bind referring to Quilting Basics. The photographed quilt was quilted with an allover paisley design. ●

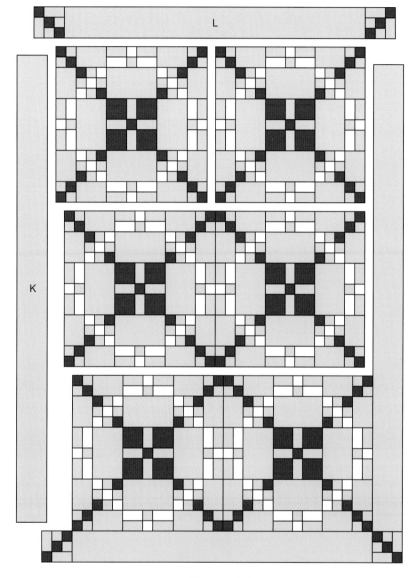

Noel Surrounded
Assembly Diagram 54" x 76½"

Kitties in the Tree

Customize your version of this quilt with kitties the colors of your own furry friends!

SKILL LEVEL
Confident Beginner

FINISHED SIZES
Quilt Size: 37" x 43"
Block Size: 4" x 6"
Number of Blocks: 6

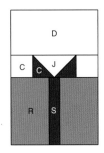

Small Gift
4" x 6" Finished Block
Make 4

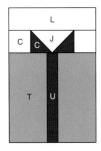

Large Gift
4" x 6" Finished Block
Make 2

MATERIALS
- 1⅛ yards ivory solid*
- ⅛ yard each of green/red diagonal stripe, green print #1, black tone-on-tone, pink print #1, pink print #2, aqua tone-on-tone and red print*
- ¼ yard each of white/multicolored print, green print #2 and green print #3*
- ½ yard each of pink dot and aqua print*
- 2½ yards backing*
- 42" x 51" batting*
- Thread*
- Basic sewing tools and supplies

*Fabrics from the Kitty Christmas collection by Urban Chiks for Moda Fabrics; Tuscany Silk batting from Hobbs Bonded Fibers; 50 wt. thread from Aurifil used to make sample. EQ8 was used to design this quilt.

PROJECT NOTES

Read all instructions before beginning this project.

Stitch right sides together using a ¼" seam allowance unless otherwise specified.

Materials and cutting lists assume 40" of usable fabric width for yardage.

Arrows indicate directions to press seams.

WOF – width of fabric

HST – half-square triangle

QST – quarter-square triangle

CUTTING

From ivory solid cut:
- 6 (8½") I squares
- 2 (6½" x 9½") X rectangles
- 2 (6½") B squares
- 2 (5½" x 8½") Y rectangles
- 2 (2½" x 8½") Z rectangles
- 4 (2½" x 4½") D rectangles
- 2 (2" x 36½") AA strips
- 1 (2" x 33½") BB strip
- 2 (2" x 6½") V rectangles
- 2 (1½" x 4½") L rectangles
- 6 (1½" x 2½") J rectangles
- 12 (1½") C squares

From green/red diagonal stripe cut:
- 1 (3½" x 12½") A rectangle
- 2 (2¼" x 4½") D rectangles

From green print #1 cut:
- 1 (3½" x 12½") A rectangle
- 2 (2¼" x 3½") R rectangles

From black tone-on-tone cut:
- 1 (3½" x 6½") W rectangle
- 2 (3½" x 4½") E rectangles
- 4 (1½" x 2½") J rectangles
- 4 (1½") C squares

From pink print #1 cut:
- 1 (3½" x 13½") N rectangle
- 1 (3½" x 9½") M rectangle
- 1 (2½") K square
- 1 (1½" x 4½") L rectangle

From pink print #2 cut:
- 1 (3½" x 14½") P rectangle
- 1 (3½" x 12½") A rectangle
- 1 (2½") K square
- 2 (2¼" x 3½") R rectangles
- 1 (1½" x 4½") L rectangle

From aqua tone-on-tone cut:
- 1 (2" x 33½") BB strip

From red print cut:
- 12 (1½") C squares
- 2 (1" x 4½") U rectangles
- 4 (1" x 3½") S rectangles

From white/multicolored print cut:
- 1 (5½" x 10½") G rectangle
- 1 (5½" x 6½") F rectangle
- 1 (2½" x 4½") D rectangle
- 2 (2¼" x 3½") R rectangles
- 2 (1½") C squares

From green print #2 cut:
- 1 (5½" x 12½") O rectangle
- 1 (5½" x 10½") G rectangle
- 1 (2½" x 4½") D rectangle
- 2 (1½") C squares

From green print #3 cut:
- 1 (5½" x 30½") Q rectangle
- 2 (2¼" x 3½") R rectangles

From pink dot cut:
- 1 (3½" x 20½") H rectangle
- 2 (2¼" x 4½") D rectangles
- 5 (2½" x WOF) binding strips

From aqua print cut:
- 2 (2½" x 39½") CC strips
- 2 (2½" x 37½") DD strips

COMPLETING THE UNITS & BLOCKS

1. Join the green/red diagonal stripe and green print #1 A rectangles (Figure 1a). Refer to Sew & Flip Corners and use the B squares and the pieced rectangle to make unit 1 (Figure 1b).

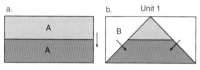

Figure 1

2. Again referring to Sew & Flip Corners, add two black C squares to the white/multicolored print D rectangle, and add two white/multicolored C squares to a black E rectangle (Figure 2a). Join the two pieced rectangles to make a cat head unit (Figure 2b).

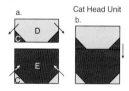

Figure 2

SEW & FLIP CORNERS

Use this method to add triangle corners in a quilt block.

1. Draw a diagonal line from corner to corner on the wrong side of the specified square. Place the square, right sides together, on the indicated corner of the larger piece, making sure the line is oriented in the correct direction indicated by the pattern (Figure 1).

Figure 1

2. Sew on the drawn line. Trim ¼" away from sewn line (Figure 2).

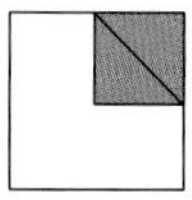

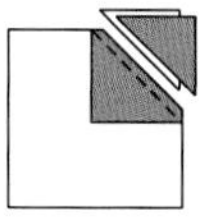

Figure 2

3. Open and press to reveal the corner triangle (Figure 3).

Figure 3

4. If desired, square up the finished unit to the required unfinished size. ●

3. Sew the white/multicolored F and G rectangles to the sides of the cat head unit as shown (Figure 3a). Add the pink dot H rectangle to the top. Using the sew-and-flip technique, add I squares to the upper corners to complete unit 2 (Figure 3b).

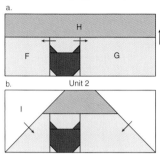

Figure 3

4. Sew black J rectangles to opposite sides of the pink print #1 K square (Figure 4). Sew the pink print #1 L rectangle to the bottom to make a paw unit.

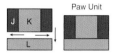

Paw Unit

Figure 4

5. Using the sew-and-flip technique, add two black C squares to the green print #2 D rectangle, and add two green print #2 C squares to a black E rectangle (Figure 5). Join the two pieced rectangles to make a cat head unit.

Cat Head Unit

Figure 5

6. Sew pink print #1 M and N rectangles to the sides of the paw unit as shown (Figure 6a). Sew green print #2 O and G rectangles to the

sides of the cat head unit. Join the pieced rectangles. Use the sew-and-flip technique and add I squares to the upper corners to complete unit 3 (Figure 6b).

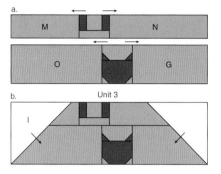

Unit 3

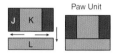

Figure 6

7. Using two black J rectangles and the pink print #2 K square and L rectangle, make a paw unit (Figure 7).

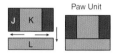

Paw Unit

Figure 7

8. Sew the pink print #2 P and A rectangles to the sides of the paw unit as shown (Figure 8a). Add the green print #3 Q rectangle to the bottom. Use the sew-and-flip technique and add I squares to the upper corners to complete unit 4 (Figure 8b).

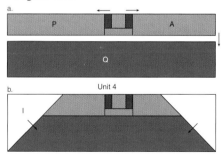

Unit 4

Figure 8

9. Using the sew-and-flip technique, add two red C squares to an ivory J rectangle (Figure 9a). Sew ivory C squares to the ends to complete a

bow unit (Figure 9b). Make six bow units.

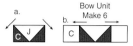

Bow Unit
Make 6

Figure 9

10. Arrange one ivory D rectangle, a bow unit, two matching print R rectangles and a red S rectangle as shown (Figure 10a). Sew the R rectangles to the S rectangle. Add the bow unit and D rectangle to the top to complete a Small Gift block (Figure 10b). Make four Small Gift blocks total.

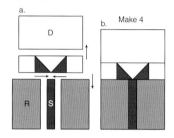

Make 4

Figure 10

11. Arrange one ivory L rectangle, a bow unit, two matching print T rectangles and a red U rectangle as shown (Figure 11a). Sew the T rectangles to the U rectangle. Add the bow unit and L rectangle to the top to complete a Large Gift block (Figure 11b). Make two Large Gift blocks total.

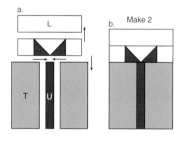

Make 2

Figure 11

12. Sew ivory V rectangles to the black W rectangle to make the trunk unit (Figure 12a and 12b).

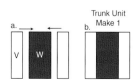

Trunk Unit
Make 1

Figure 12

COMPLETING THE QUILT

1. Referring to the Assembly Diagram, lay out the units and blocks in five rows. Add the ivory X, Y and Z rectangles to the first three rows as shown.

2. Sew the X rectangles to unit 1 to complete the first row. Add the Y and Z rectangles to units 2 and 3. Join the six gift blocks and the trunk unit as shown to complete the fifth (bottom) row. Join all five rows to complete the quilt center. Press.

3. Sew the AA–DD border strips to the quilt top in alphabetical order.
4. Layer, baste, quilt as desired and bind referring to Quilting Basics. The photographed quilt was quilted with an edge-to-edge swirling snowflakes design. ●

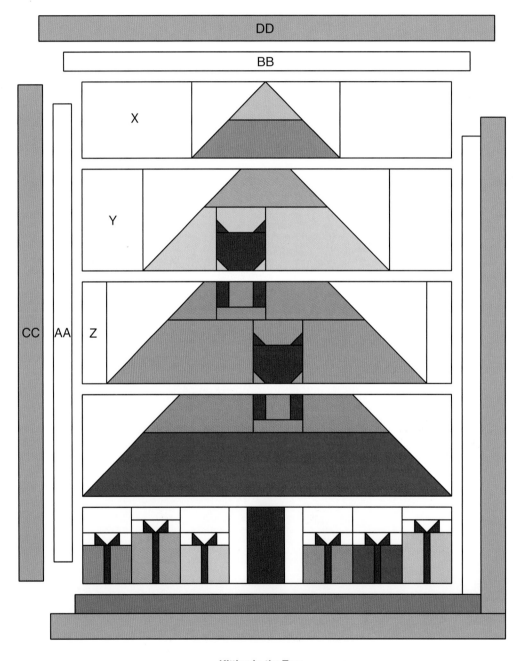

Kitties in the Tree
Assembly Diagram 37" x 43"

DESIGNED & QUILTED BY JILL METZGER

Blue Spruce

This cozy design is perfect for snuggling on cold winter nights.

SKILL LEVEL
Confident Beginner

FINISHED SIZES
Quilt Size: 56" x 56"
Block Size: 6" x 6" and 12" x 12"
Number of Blocks: 28 and 9

Four-Patch
6" x 6" Finished Block
Make 4

Large Red Pinwheel
6" x 6" Finished Block
Make 6

Large Plaid Pinwheel
6" x 6" Finished Block
Make 6

Spruce Block
6" x 6" Finished Block
Make 12

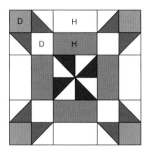

Block 1
12" x 12" Finished Block
Make 5

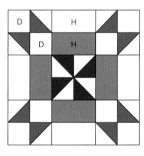

Block 2
12" x 12" Finished Block
Make 4

MATERIALS
- 2⅞ yards white solid
- ⅜ yard black check
- ½ yard red print
- ¾ yard red plaid
- ¾ yard green print
- ⅛ yard black print
- ⅝ yard green/black check
- ⅝ yard black solid
- 3⅞ yards backing
- 64" x 64" batting
- Thread
- Basic sewing tools and supplies

PROJECT NOTES
Read all instructions before beginning this project.

Stitch right sides together using a ¼" seam allowance unless otherwise specified.

Materials and cutting lists assume 40" of usable fabric width for yardage.

Arrows indicate directions to press seams.

WOF – width of fabric

HST – half-square triangle

QST – quarter-square triangle

CUTTING

From white solid cut:
- 6 (8") B squares
- 20 (6") C squares
- 8 (3½") A squares
- 24 (2½" x 3⅛") F rectangles
- 8 (2½" x 6½") I rectangles
- 36 (2½" x 4½") H rectangles
- 52 (2½") D squares
- 5 (2½" x WOF) strips, stitch short ends to short ends, then subcut into:
    2 (2½" x 36½") J border strips
    2 (2½" x 40½") K border strips
- 24 (1½" x 2½") E rectangles

From black check cut:
- 8 (3½") A squares
- 20 (2½") D squares

From red print cut:
- 3 (8") B squares
- 5 (6") C squares

From red plaid cut:
- 3 (8") B squares
- 36 (2½" x 4½") H rectangles

From green print cut:
- 15 (6") C squares
- 12 (2½") D squares

From black print cut:
- 12 (1¼" x 2½") G rectangles

From green/black check cut:
- 6 (2½" x WOF) strips, stitch short ends to short ends, then subcut into:
  2 (2½" x 52½") L border strips
  2 (2½" x 56½") M border strips

From black solid cut:
- 7 (2½" x WOF) binding strips

COMPLETING THE BLOCKS

1. Lay out two white A squares and 2 black check A squares. Join as shown to complete a Four-Patch block (Figure 1). Make four.

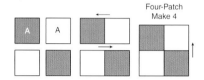

Figure 1

2. Referring to Eight-at-a-Time Half-Square Triangles, use white B squares and red print B squares to make 24 large red HSTs. Repeat to make 24 large plaid HSTs using white B squares and red plaid B squares. Similarly, use white C squares and red C squares to make 40 small red

HSTs (four are extra); use white C squares and green print C squares to make 120 small green HSTs (Figure 2).

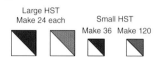

Figure 2

3. Lay out four large red HSTs. Join to make a Large Red Pinwheel block. Make six. Repeat to make six Large Plaid Pinwheel blocks and nine small red pinwheels (Figure 3). Set the small red pinwheels aside for Blocks 1 and 2 assembly.

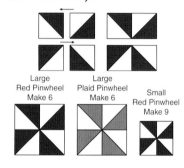

Figure 3

4. Lay out two white E rectangles, two white F rectangles, four small green HSTs, one green D square and

one black print G rectangle. Join into rows, then join rows to complete a Spruce block (Figure 4). Make 12.

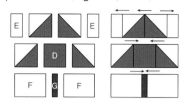

Figure 4

5. Lay out one white D square, one black check D square and two small green HSTs. Join as shown to make a corner unit 1 (Figure 5). Make 20. Similarly, use two white D squares and two small green HSTs to make a corner unit 2. Make 16.

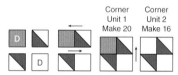

Figure 5

EIGHT-AT-A-TIME HALF-SQUARE TRIANGLES

Half-square triangles (HSTs) are a basic unit of quilting used in many blocks or on their own. This construction method will yield eight HST units.

1. Refer to the pattern for size to cut squares. The standard formula is to add 1" to the finished size of the square then multiply by 2. Cut two squares from different colors this size. For example, for a 3" finished HST unit, cut 8" squares (3" + 1" = 4"; 4" x 2 = 8").

2. Draw two diagonal lines from corner to corner on the wrong side of the lightest color square. Layer the squares

right sides together. Stitch ¼" on either side of both drawn lines (Figure A).

Figure A

3. Cut the sewn squares in half horizontally and vertically, making four squares. Then cut each square apart on the drawn line, leaving a ¼" seam allowance and making eight HST units referring to Figure B. Trim each HST unit to the desired size (3½" in this example).

Figure B

4. Open the HST units and press seam allowances toward the darker fabric making eight HST units (Figure C). ●

Figure C

6. Join one white H rectangle and one plaid H rectangle to make a side unit (Figure 6). Make 36.

Side Unit
Make 36

H

H

Figure 6

7. Lay out one small red pinwheel, four corner unit 1s, and four side units. Join as shown to complete Block 1 (Figure 7). Make five. In the same way, make four Block 2s using small red pinwheels, corner unit 2s and side units.

COMPLETING THE QUILT

1. Referring to the Assembly Diagram, lay out Blocks 1 and 2 in alternating rows of three. Join as shown. Add the white J and K strips.
2. Sew Four-Patch, Large Red Pinwheel, Large Plaid Pinwheel and Spruce blocks, and white I rectangles to make top and bottom rows. Then sew Large Red Pinwheel, Large Plaid Pinwheel and Spruce blocks, and white I rectangles to make two side rows. Add the side rows first, then add top and bottom rows.
3. Sew the green/black L and M border strips to the quilt center.
4. Layer, baste, quilt as desired and bind referring to Quilting Basics. The photographed quilt was quilted stitch-in-the-ditch along the seams. ●

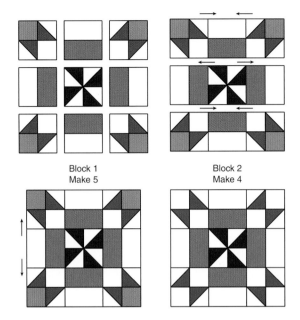

Block 1
Make 5

Block 2
Make 4

Figure 7

Blue Spruce
Assembly Diagram 56" x 56"

Good Tidings

Cool winter blues provide a calming elegance in this snowy sky design.

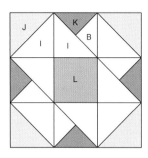

X
12" x 12" Finished Block
Make 18

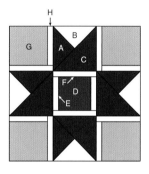

Star
12" x 12" Finished Block
Make 17

MATERIALS
- ⅓ yard red swirl*
- ⅜ yard aqua leaves*
- ⅝ yard light blue snowflake*
- ⅝ yard aqua swirl for binding*
- 1 yard aqua snowflake*
- 1⅛ yards aqua dot*
- 1½ yards blue floral*
- 3⅝ yards white dot*
- 5½ yards backing fabric*
- 74" x 98" batting
- Thread
- Basic sewing tools and supplies

Fabric from Island Batik used to make sample.

SKILL LEVEL
Confident Beginner

FINISHED SIZES
Quilt Size: 64" x 88"
Block Size: 12" x 12"
Number of Blocks: 35

PROJECT NOTES
Read all instructions before beginning this project.

Stitch right sides together using a ¼" seam allowance unless otherwise specified.

Arrows indicate directions to press seams.

Materials and cutting lists assume 40" of usable fabric width for yardage.
WOF – width of fabric
HST – half-square triangle
QST – quarter-square triangle

CUTTING

From red swirl cut:
- 17 (3½") D squares

From aqua leaves cut:
- 18 (4½") L squares

From light blue snowflake cut:
- 18 (5½") K squares

From aqua swirl cut:
- 8 (2¼" x WOF) binding strips

From aqua snowflake cut:
- 68 (4") G squares

From aqua dot cut:
- 36 (5½") J squares

From blue floral cut:
- 17 (5½") A squares
- 34 (5") C squares

From white dot cut:
- 35 (5½") B squares
- 72 (5") I squares
- 8 (2½" x WOF) strips, stitch short ends to short ends, then subcut into:
  2 (2½" x 84½") M and 2 (2½" x 64½") N strips
- 102 (1" x 4½") F rectangles
- 68 (1" x 4") H rectangles
- 34 (1" x 3½") E rectangles

COMPLETING THE BLOCKS

1. Refer to Half-Square Triangles on page 31 to make HST units using A and B squares (Figure 1). Do not trim units. Make 34 A-B units.

A-B Unit
Make 34

Figure 1

2. Draw a diagonal line on the wrong side of one A-B unit, perpendicular to the seam (Figure 2). Pair with one C square and refer to Half-Square Triangles to make two star point units. Trim to measure 4½" square. Make 68.

Star Point Units
Make 68

Figure 2

3. Sew E rectangles to opposite sides of one D square. Sew F rectangles to the top and bottom to make a center unit (Figure 3). Make 17.

Center Unit
Make 17

Figure 3

4. Sew one H rectangle to the right side a G square. Sew one F rectangle to the bottom to make one corner unit (Figure 4). Make 68.

Corner Unit
Make 68

Figure 4

5. Lay out four star point units, four corner units and one center unit into three rows (Figure 5). Sew into rows and join the rows to make a Star block. Make 17.

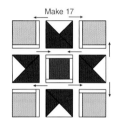

Make 17

Figure 5

6. Refer to Half-Square Triangles to make HST units using B and K squares (Figure 6). Do not trim units. Make 36 B-K units. In the same way, make 72 I-J units using I and J squares and trim to measure 4½" square.

B-K Unit
Make 36

I-J Unit
Make 72

Figure 6

7. Draw a diagonal line on the wrong side of one B-K unit, perpendicular to the seam (Figure 7). Pair with one I square and refer to Half-Square Triangles to make two B-K-I units. Trim to measure 4½" square. Make 72.

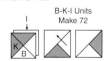

B-K-I Units
Make 72

Figure 7

8. Lay out four B-K-I units, four I-J units and one L square into three rows (Figure 8). Sew into rows and join the rows to make an X block. Make 18.

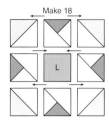

Make 18

Figure 8

COMPLETING THE QUILT

1. Lay out Star blocks alternating with X blocks into seven rows of five blocks each. Sew blocks into rows and join the rows to complete the quilt center.

2. Sew M strips to opposite sides of the quilt center. Sew N strips to the top and bottom to complete the quilt.

3. Layer, baste, quilt as desired and bind referring to Quilting Basics. The photographed quilt was quilted with a wavy line grid design. ●

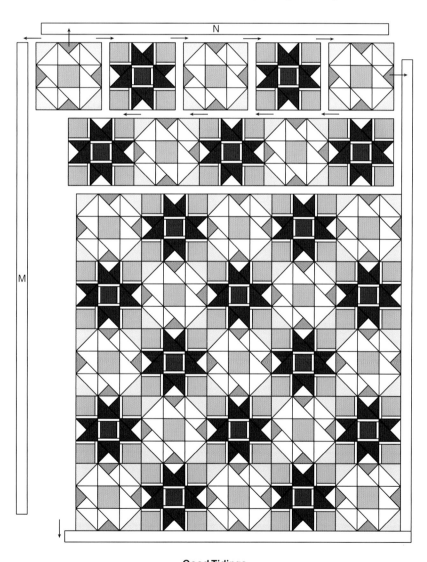

Good Tidings
Assembly Diagram 64" x 88"

Ribbon Curls Runner

This creative runner pays homage to fun family gift wrapping traditions.

SKILL LEVEL
Confident Beginner

FINISHED SIZES
Table Runner Size: 45½" x 14½"
Block Size: 3½" x 3½"
Number of Blocks: 30

MATERIALS
- ⅞ yard cream print*
- ⅜ yard green print*
- ⅜ yard red gingham*
- ¼ yard red print*
- ⅜ yard green gingham*
- ½ yard dark green blender*
- 1½ yards backing*
- 18" x 50" batting
- Thread
- Basic sewing tools and supplies

Fabric from the Homemade Holiday collection by Kris Lammers for Maywood Studio used to make sample.

PROJECT NOTES
Read all instructions before beginning this project.

Stitch right sides together using a ¼" seam allowance unless otherwise specified.

Materials and cutting lists assume 40" of usable fabric width for yardage.

Arrows indicate directions to press seams.

WOF – width of fabric
HST – half-square triangle
QST – quarter-square triangle

CUTTING

From cream print cut:
- 5 (4¾") B squares, then cut twice diagonally (two triangles are extra)
- 6 (4⅜") A squares, then cut once diagonally
- 2 (4") C squares
- 1 (4" x 25") D rectangle
- 3 (2½" x WOF) strips, stitch short ends to short ends, then subcut into:
    2 (2½" x 45½") E border strips

From green print cut:
- 3 (4¾") B squares, then cut twice diagonally (three triangles are extra)
- 2 (4⅜") A squares, then cut once diagonally (one triangle is extra)

From red gingham cut:
- 2 (4¾") B squares, then cut twice diagonally (one triangle is extra)
- 3 (4⅜") A squares, then cut once diagonally (one triangle is extra)

From red print cut:
- 6 (4⅜") A squares, then cut once diagonally

From green gingham cut:
- 1 (4¾") B square, then cut twice diagonally (two triangles are extra)
- 5 (4⅜") A squares, then cut once diagonally

From dark green blender cut:
- 4 (2½" x WOF) binding strips

"*Are you ready to curl some ribbons, patchwork style? One of my fondest childhood memories was curling up ribbons for bows on Christmas gifts. I enjoyed holding the scissors against the ribbon and watching the ringlets appear as I ran the blade across the surface. By mixing the half-square triangles and split half-square triangle units you can create a patchwork that appears to twist across the surface of the runner. Fun fact: I have always had curly hair, which may be why I loved making these kinds of bows for all our gifts. My family and friends always knew which packages were from me.*" —Michelle Freedman

COMPLETING THE HST UNITS

Starch fabric well with a spray starch to avoid excess stretch for triangles cut on the bias.

1. Place a cream A triangle over a green A triangle, right sides together. Stitch ¼" away from long edge. Open and press to make HST unit. Make three (Figure 1).

HST
Make 3

Figure 1

2. Repeat to make three cream/red gingham HST units, three cream/red HST units and three cream/green gingham HST units (Figure 2).

Make 3 each

Figure 2

3. Lay out one cream B triangle, one red gingham B triangle and one red A triangle. Join as shown to make a split HST unit (Figure 3). Make seven.

Split HST
Make 7

Figure 3

4. Repeat to make two cream B/green B/red gingham A split HST units, two cream B/green gingham B/red A split

HST units and seven cream B/green B/green gingham A split HST units (Figure 4).

Make 2 Make 2 Make 7

Figure 4

COMPLETING THE TABLE RUNNER

1. Referring to the Assembly Diagram, lay out the units, cream C squares, cream D rectangle, and cream E border strips as shown.

2. Sew into rows and join the rows to complete the table runner top. Press.

3. Layer, baste, quilt as desired and bind referring to Quilting Basics. The photographed table runner was quilted with a walking foot grid pattern that followed the angles of the "ribbons." ●

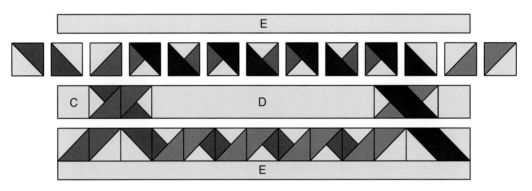

Ribbon Curls Runner
Assembly Diagram 14½" x 45½"

DESIGNED & QUILTED BY JOY HEIMARK

Celestial Stars

Three Star blocks are surrounded by partial log cabins and borders to make this attractive runner. The blue fabrics give it a crisp, clean look.

SKILL LEVEL
Confident Beginner

FINISHED SIZES
Table Runner Size: 58" x 24"
Block Size: 12" x 12"
Number of Blocks: 3

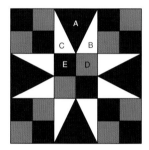

Star
12" x 12" Finished Block
Make 3

MATERIALS
- ¼ yard white solid
- ⅜ yard light print
- ⅜ yard pale blue print
- ⅜ yard medium blue print
- ⅝ yard navy blue print
- 1 yard blue floral
- 1⅞ yards backing fabric
- 30" x 64" batting
- Thread
- Basic sewing tools and supplies
- Plastic template material

PROJECT NOTES
Read all instructions before beginning this project.

Stitch right sides together using a ¼" seam allowance unless otherwise specified.

Arrows indicate directions to press seams.

Materials and cutting lists assume 40" of usable fabric width for yardage.
WOF – width of fabric
HST – half-square triangle
QST – quarter-square triangle

CUTTING

From white solid cut:
- 12 B pieces from template
- 12 C pieces from template

From light print cut:
- 12 (2½" x 10½") H rectangles

From pale blue print cut:
- 24 (2½") F squares
- 3 (1" x WOF) strips, stitch short ends to short ends, then subcut into:
  2 (1" x 51½") I strips
- 2 (1" x 18½") J strips

From medium blue print cut:
- 12 (2½" x 6½") G rectangles
- 30 (2½") D squares

From navy blue print cut:
- 12 A pieces from template
- 42 (2½") E squares
- 3 (1" x WOF) strips, stitch short ends to short ends, then subcut into:
  2 (1" x 52½") K strips
- 2 (1" x 19½") L strips

From blue floral cut:
- 4 (3" x WOF) strips, stitch short ends to short ends, then subcut into:
  2 (3" x 53½") M and 2 (3" x 24½") N strips
- 5 (2¼" x WOF) binding strips

COMPLETING THE BLOCKS

1. Sew one each B and C pieces to opposite sides of one A piece to make a star point unit (Figure 1). Make 12.

Star Point Unit
Make 12

Figure 1

2. Arrange two each D and E squares into two rows. Sew into rows and join to make one D-E unit (Figure 2). Make 15.

D-E Unit
Make 15

Figure 2

3. Lay out four star point units and five D-E units into three rows. Sew into rows and join the rows to make a Star block (Figure 3). Make three.

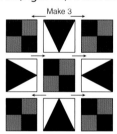

Figure 3

4. Sew one E square to the left side of one F square. Sew one E square below the F square to make one E-F unit (Figure 4). Make four.

E-F Unit
Make 4

Figure 4

5. Sew one G rectangle to the top of one E-F unit. Sew one F square to the end of a second G rectangle, and then sew to the right side of the E-F unit (Figure 5). Make four.

E-F-G Unit
Make 4

Figure 5

6. Sew one H rectangle to the top of one E-F-G unit. Sew one F square to the end of a second H rectangle and then sew to the right side of the E-F-G unit to make one half log cabin unit (Figure 6). Make four.

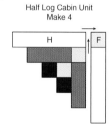

Half Log Cabin Unit
Make 4

Figure 6

7. Join one each E and F squares to make one E-F unit (Figure 7). Join one F square to one G rectangle to make one F-G unit. Sew one F square to one H rectangle to make one F-H unit. Make four each.

F-G Unit   F-H Unit
Make 4 each

Figure 7

8. Sew together one each E-F, F-G and F-H unit as shown, making sure each F square extends ¼" past the seam line of the adjoining unit to make a corner unit (Figure 8). Make two.

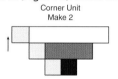

Corner Unit
Make 2

Figure 8

9. In the same way, make two corner units in reverse (Figure 9).

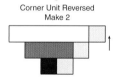

Corner Unit Reversed
Make 2

Figure 9

COMPLETING THE RUNNER

1. Lay out Star blocks, half log cabin units, corner units and corner units reversed into five diagonal rows. Sew into rows and join the rows to complete the runner center.

2. Trim runner ¼" past the block points on all four sides (Figure 10).

¼"

Figure 10

3. Sew border strips to the runner center in alphabetical order to complete the runner.

4. Layer, baste, quilt as desired and bind referring to Quilting Basics. The photographed table runner was quilted with an overall meandering design. ●

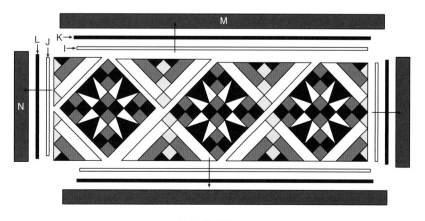

Celestial Stars
Assembly Diagram 58" x 24"

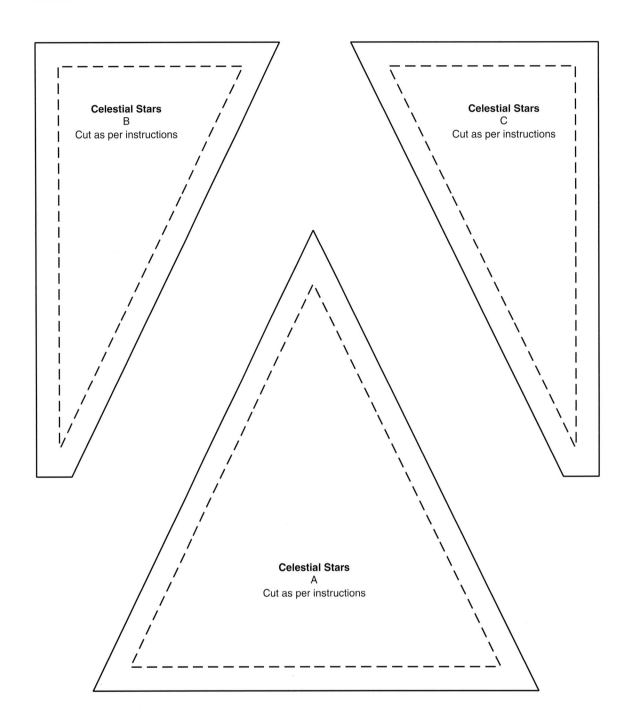

Celestial Stars
B
Cut as per instructions

Celestial Stars
C
Cut as per instructions

Celestial Stars
A
Cut as per instructions

DESIGNED & QUILTED BY RACHELLE CRAIG

Winter Morning

Create a wintry runner that can adorn your table all season.

SKILL LEVEL
Confident Beginner

FINISHED SIZES
Table Runner Size: 43" x 16"
Block Size: 9" x 9"
Number of Blocks: 3

Winter Morning
9" x 9" Finished Block
Make 3

MATERIALS
- ¼ yard light blue tonal*
- ⅛ yard medium blue tonal*
- ⅝ yard dark blue tonal*
- ⅞ yard navy tonal*
- 1¼ yards backing*
- 20" x 47" batting*
- Thread
- Basic sewing tools and supplies

Fabric from the Cotton Shot collection by Amanda Murphy for Benartex; Tuscany Wool/Cotton Blend batting from Hobbs Bonded Fibers used to make sample.

PROJECT NOTES
Read all instructions before beginning this project.

Stitch right sides together using a ¼" seam allowance unless otherwise specified.

Materials and cutting lists assume 42" of usable fabric width for yardage.

Arrows indicate directions to press seams.

WOF – width of fabric
HST – half-square triangle
QST – quarter-square triangle

CUTTING

From light blue tonal cut:
- 3 (4½") A squares
- 12 (2") C squares

From medium blue tonal cut:
- 12 (2¾") B squares

From dark blue tonal cut:
- 6 (4½") A squares
- 3 (3½") F squares
- 3 (2½" x WOF) binding strips

From navy tonal cut:
- 1 (14") E square, cut twice diagonally
- 2 (7¼") D squares, cut once diagonally
- 3 (4½") A squares
- 1 (3½") F square, cut once diagonally
- 12 (2¾") B squares
- 12 (2") C squares
- 2 (1½" x WOF) G strips

COMPLETING THE BLOCKS

1. Refer to Half-Square Triangles on page 31 and use light blue and dark blue A squares to make six light/dark HST (Figure 1).

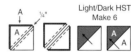

Figure 1

2. In the same way, use dark blue and navy A squares to make six dark/navy HST (Figure 2).

Figure 2

3. In the same manner, use light/dark and dark/navy HST to make 12 QST (Figure 3). Trim to 3½".

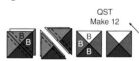

Figure 3

4. Using the Half-Square Triangles method, use medium blue and navy B squares to make 24 medium/navy HST (Figure 4). Trim to 2".

Figure 4

5. Sew a navy C square, a light blue C square and two medium/navy HST into rows; join rows (Figure 5). Make 12.

Figure 5

"I wanted to capture the peace and stillness of an evening snow as the flakes drift slowly toward the ground against the darkening sky." —Rachelle Craig

6. Sew four step 5 units, four QST and a dark blue F square into three rows; join rows to complete a Winter Morning block (Figure 6). Make three.

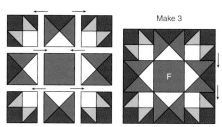

Make 3

Figure 6

COMPLETING THE TABLE RUNNER

1. Referring to the Assembly Diagram, lay out Winter Morning blocks, D triangles and E triangles in diagonal rows as shown.

2. Sew the blocks into rows; join rows. Trim setting triangles to ¼" beyond the tips of the blocks to complete the table runner center.

3. Sew F triangles to short ends of runner, centering them vertically. Sew the G border strips to the long sides; trim square with side edges.

4. Trim short ends on the diagonal 1½" beyond the diagonal edges of the end blocks as shown.

5. Layer, baste, quilt as desired and bind referring to Quilting Basics. The photographed table runner was quilted with diagonal serpentine lines. ●

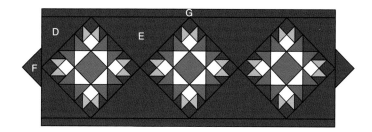

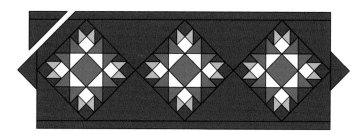

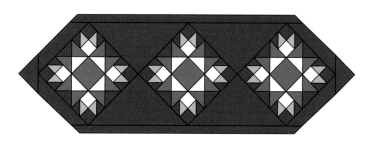

Winter Morning
Assembly Diagram 43" x 16"

HALF-SQUARE TRIANGLES

Half-square triangles (HSTs) are a basic unit of quilting used in many blocks or on their own. This construction method will yield two HSTs.

1. Refer to the pattern for size to cut squares. The standard formula is to add ⅞" to the finished size of the square. Cut two squares from different colors this size. For example, for a 3" finished HST unit, cut 3⅞" squares.

2. Draw a diagonal line from corner to corner on the wrong side of the lightest color square. Layer the squares right sides together. Stitch ¼" on either side of the drawn line (Figure A).

Figure A

3. Cut the squares apart on the drawn line, leaving a ¼" seam allowance and making two HST units referring to Figure B.

Figure B

4. Open the HST units and press seam allowances toward the darker fabric making two HST units (Figure C). ●

Figure C

Little Tree Basket

This project goes together quickly and makes a wonderful gift basket. Fill it with baked goods, small items or maybe a pretty poinsettia.

SKILL LEVEL
Confident Beginner

FINISHED SIZE
Basket Size: 6" x 6" x 5"

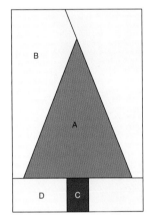

Tree
3" x 4½" Finished Block
Make 2

MATERIALS
- Fat quarter or ⅓ yard dark green plaid
- Fat quarter or ⅓ yard cream print
- Small piece each dark green, dark red and brown tonals
- ½ yard 20"-wide heavy-weight interfacing, one-side fusible
- 2 small star buttons
- Template material
- Thread
- Basic sewing tools and supplies

PROJECT NOTES
Read all instructions before beginning this project.

Stitch right sides together using a ¼" seam allowance unless otherwise specified.

Materials and cutting lists assume 40" of usable fabric width for yardage and 20" for fat quarters.

Arrows indicate directions to press seams.

WOF – width of fabric
HST – half-square triangle ◻
QST – quarter-square triangle ⊠

CUTTING

From green plaid cut:
- 2 (1¼" x 3½") E rectangles
- 2 (3½"x 3¾") F rectangles
- 4 (4½" x 9") G rectangles

From cream print cut:
- 2 (9½" x 11½") I rectangles
- 4 (1¼" x 1¾") D rectangles

From dark red tonal cut:
- 2 (2½" x 6") H rectangles

From brown tonal cut:
- 2 (1" x 1¼") C rectangles

From interfacing cut:
- 2 (9" x 11½") rectangles

COMPLETING THE BLOCKS
1. Using the patterns provided, cut the following shapes:
- Dark green tonal: 2 A shapes
- Cream print: 2 each B and BR shapes

Here's a Tip

Place the template made from the B shape facedown on the right side of the fabric to cut the BR shape.

2. Arrange one B triangle and one A triangle as shown, offsetting bottom of B triangle ¼" from bottom corner of A triangle (Figure 1). Sew triangles together and press. Make two.

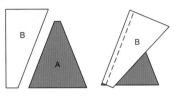

Figure 1

3. In the same manner, sew one BR triangle to the right side of one step 1 unit; trim seam allowance to ¼" and press to make one tree top unit (Figure 2). Trim tree top unit to 3½" x 4¼". Make two.

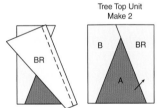

Figure 2

4. Sew two D rectangles to opposite long sides of one C rectangle to make one tree trunk unit (Figure 3). Make two.

Tree Trunk Unit
Make 2

Figure 3

5. Referring to the Tree block diagram, sew together one tree top unit and one tree trunk unit to complete one Tree block. Make two.

COMPLETING THE BASKET

1. Sew one E rectangle to the top of a Tree block and an F rectangle to the bottom (Figure 4). Sew a G rectangle to each side to complete one basket front/back unit. Make two.

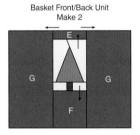

Basket Front/Back Unit
Make 2

Figure 4

2. Fuse one interfacing rectangle to the wrong side of each basket front/back unit following the manufacturer's instructions. Quilt as desired. The photographed basket is stitched in the ditch along the seam lines and with a 1" vertical grid.
3. Referring to the Placement Diagram, sew a star button to the top of each tree.
4. Cut out a 2½" square from the bottom corners of each basket front/back unit (Figure 5).

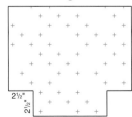

Figure 5

5. Place the two basket front/back units together, right sides facing, and stitch together along the side and bottom edges (Figure 6). Press seams open.

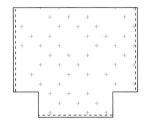

Figure 6

6. Match the side and bottom seams on the cutout corners and sew to box the corners (Figure 7). Turn basket right side out.

Figure 7

7. To make the handles, fold an H rectangle in half lengthwise, right sides together, and sew the long edges together. Turn right side out and press edges flat; topstitch ¼" from both long edges. Make two.
8. Position the handles on the sides of the basket, placing each handle end ½" from the side seam as shown (Figure 8). Stitch across the handle ends to secure. Repeat for second handle.

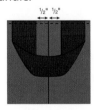

Figure 8

9. Repeat steps 4–6 with the I rectangles to make the basket lining. Do not turn the basket lining right side out.

10. Press a ¼" hem at the top of the lining. Push the lining into the basket, aligning side seams. Fold the lining over the top front of the basket about ⅜". Use a small slip stitch to sew the folded edges to the basket, being careful not to stitch through the lining inside the basket to complete the basket (Figure 9). ●

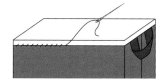

Figure 9

Here's a Tip

The basket model has a matching Tree block on the front and on the back. If you prefer, you can eliminate the block on the back and use a 9" x 11½" green plaid rectangle for the back.

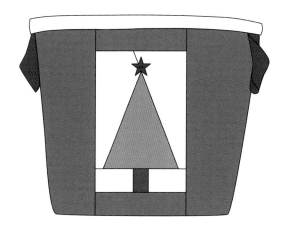

Little Tree Basket
Placement Diagram 6" x 6" x 5"

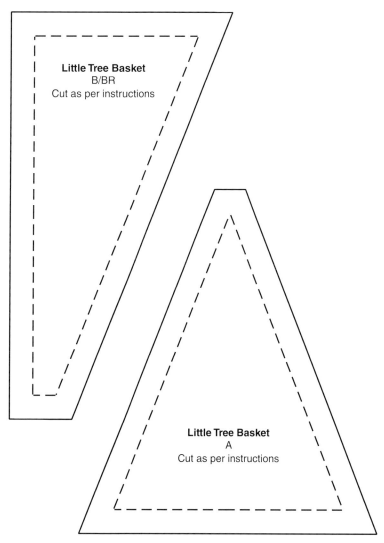

Little Tree Basket
B/BR
Cut as per instructions

Little Tree Basket
A
Cut as per instructions

DESIGN BY CHRIS MALONE

Santa Tote

This fun tote is large enough to accommodate a long day of shopping or can be used as a much-appreciated gift bag.

SKILL LEVEL
Confident Beginner

FINISHED SIZE
Tote Bag Size: 14" x 14" x 4"

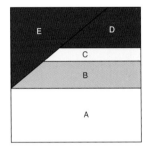

Santa
10" x 10" Finished Block
Make 1

MATERIALS
- ⅞ yard green stripe
- ⅝ yard red stripe
- Fat eighth or ⅓ yard red print
- Fat eighth or ¼ yard white tonal
- Small piece pink tonal
- Small strip white with red text print
- 21" x 40" batting*
- 2 (⅝"-diameter) black buttons
- 1 (1⅛"-diameter) cover button kit
- 1 (1½"-diameter) white pompom
- Fabric glue
- Thread*
- Basic sewing tools and supplies

*Warm and Natural Cotton Batting from The Warm Company; 50 wt. Cotton thread from Aurifil used to make sample.

PROJECT NOTES
Read all instructions before beginning this project.

Stitch right sides together using a ¼" seam allowance unless otherwise specified.

Materials and cutting lists assume 40" of usable fabric width for yardage and 20" for fat eighths.

Arrows indicate directions to press seams.

WOF – width of fabric

HST – half-square triangle

QST – quarter-square triangle

CUTTING

From green stripe cut:
Note: If using striped fabric, cut so all the pieces have vertical stripes.
- 1 (17" x 19½") I rectangle
- 2 (5" x 17") H rectangles
- 1 (5" x 10½") G rectangle
- 1 (2½" x 10½") F strip
- 2 (1¾" x 15") J strips

From red stripe cut:
- 2 (17" x 19½") L rectangles
- 2 (1¾" x 15") K strips

From red print cut:
- 1 (8") E square
- 1 (3½" x 10½") D strip

From white tonal cut:
- 1 (4½" x 10½") A strip

From pink tonal cut:
- 1 (2½" x 1½") B strip

From white with red text print cut:
- 1 (1½" x 10½") C strip

From batting cut:
- 2 (17" x 19½") tote body rectangles (tote front and back)
- 1 (3¼" x 7½") appliqué rectangle (mustache)
- 2 (1¾" x 15") handle strips (handles)

Here's a Tip

For a firmer tote, use a sew-in foam stabilizer.

COMPLETING THE BLOCK

1. Sew the A, B, C and D strips together as shown, with A at the bottom and D at the top (Figure 1).

Figure 1

2. On the back of the E square, mark a point 6" down from the top left corner and draw a diagonal line from the marked point to the top right corner (Figure 2).

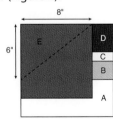

Figure 2

3. Referring to Sew & Flip Corners on page 11 and the Santa block diagram, sew the E square to the top left corner of the step 1 unit. Press the E square open and trim the edges even at the corner to complete the Santa block.

COMPLETING THE TOTE

1. Sew the F strip to the top of the Santa block and the G rectangle to the bottom of the block as shown (Figure 3). Sew the H rectangles to the sides to complete the tote front.

Tote Front

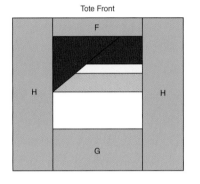

Figure 3

2. Baste one tote body batting rectangle to the wrong side of the tote front and quilt as desired. Repeat with the I rectangle for the tote back. The photographed tote was quilted along the seam lines inside the Santa block and with swirls in the beard area and finished with a 1" vertical grid.

3. Cut a 2½" square from the bottom corners of each quilted step 2 unit as shown (Figure 4).

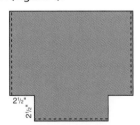

Figure 4

4. Pin the tote front to the quilted I rectangle, right sides facing, and stitch the bottom and side seams. Press seams open.

5. Fold the bottom seam to the adjacent side seam, right sides facing and matching seam lines, and stitch a ¼" seam to box the corners (Figure 5). Repeat with remaining corner. Turn tote right side out.

Figure 5

6. Pair each J strip with a K strip, right sides facing, and pin to a handle batting strip (Figure 6). Sew along both long edges, trim the batting close to the seam and turn handles right side out. Press edges flat and topstitch ¼" from the long edges.

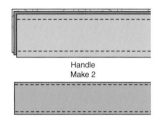

Handle
Make 2

Figure 6

7. Pin the ends of one handle to the tote front, centered on the top edge of the tote with the green side down and 5" between the handle ends (Figure 7). Stitch across the handle ends. Repeat with the remaining handle along the top edge of the tote back.

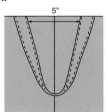

Figure 7

8. Referring to Padded Appliqué and Figure 8, prepare mustache template using pattern provided and make one mustache from white tonal fabric and batting appliqué rectangle (Figure 8a). Topstitch close to the outside edge of the mustache (Figure 8b).

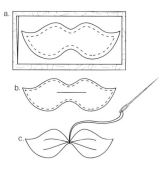

Figure 8

9. Using a doubled length of white thread, sew a gathering stitch up the center of the mustache (Figure 8c). Pull threads to gather the center of the mustache, wrap the threads around the center several times and knot, leaving the thread tails.

10. Following the manufacturer's directions, cover the button with a scrap of the pink tonal to make the button nose.

11. Referring to the Placement Diagram, tack the mustache to the center of the Santa face at the A-B seam, then add button nose and the black buttons to the Santa face as shown.

12. To make the lining, repeat steps 3 and 4 using the L rectangles and leaving a 6" opening along the bottom seam. Repeat step 5 to box the corners of the lining. Do not turn the lining right side out.

13. Slip the tote inside the lining, matching the side seams; pin and sew all around the top edge of the tote. Turn the tote right side out through the opening in the bottom of the lining. Fold in the seam allowance on the lining opening and slip stitch the folded edge together. Push the lining inside the tote and press the top edges flat.

14. With the handles pulled up, topstitch ¼" from the edge around the top edge of the tote.

15. Glue the pompom to the tip of the Santa hat as shown to finish tote. ●

Santa Tote
Placement Diagram 14" x 14" x 4"

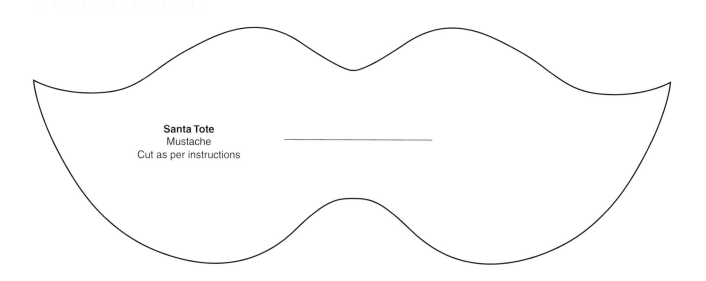

Santa Tote
Mustache
Cut as per instructions

PADDED APPLIQUÉ

Padded appliqué is a technique used to add dimensional interest to a project. The appliqué is made with two layers of fabric and one layer of batting stitched together and then turned right side out through an opening or slash.

1. Transfer patterns to template material and cut out. Transfer all markings, especially those for slashes and openings.

2. Using templates, trace shape onto wrong side of selected fabric as many times as indicated in pattern as shown in Figure A. Transfer all markings to fabric.

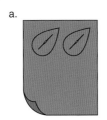

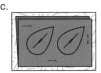

Figure A

3. Cut a small opening along slash markings. Do not cut entire length open.

4. Fold fabric in half with right sides together and with traced shapes on top as shown in Figure A.

5. Pin fabric to slightly larger batting scrap, referring again to Figure A.

6. Follow project and template instructions to either stitch completely around the shape or stitch leaving an opening for turning as shown in Figure B.

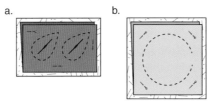

Figure B

7. Cut out shape ⅛"–¼" from stitching line. Trim layers close to stitching and clip seam allowance curves being careful not to clip through stitching line as shown in Figure C. Or use pinking shears to trim close to seam, eliminating the need for other trimming or clipping seam allowances.

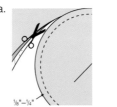

Figure C

8. If cutting a slash in appliqué, insert scissors in previously made opening along slash mark and cut indicated slash as shown in Figure D. Apply no-fray solution to cut edges if desired.

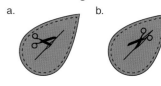

Figure D

9. Turn appliqué right side out through slash or opening as shown in Figure E.

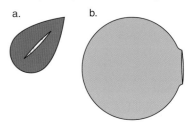

Figure E

10. Turn seam allowance to inside if opening has been left. Press appliqués flat.

11. Whipstitch openings or slashes closed.

12. Topstitch and/or quilt and apply to project as indicated in pattern instructions to complete. ●

DESIGN BY CHRIS MALONE

Gingerbread Love Garland

Make this sweet garland to hang on the mantel or across a buffet or kitchen cabinet for a cheerful decoration! It combines fusible appliquéd pennants with hand-stitched wool felt ornaments.

SKILL LEVEL
Confident Beginner

FINISHED SIZES
Garland Size: 8" x 70"
Pennant Size: 6" x 8"
Ornament Size: 3⅝" x 3¼"

MATERIALS
- ⅔ yard red dot
- ¼ yard brown tonal
- Small piece each square pink dot and red/white stripe
- 5 (7" x 9") batting rectangles
- 2 (9" x 12") sheets white wool felt
- 5" square red wool felt
- 1 yard (¼"-wide) white rickrack
- 10 (³⁄₁₆"-diameter) white buttons
- 4 (¾"-diameter) white buttons
- 2 (½"-diameter) white buttons
- 5 (³⁄₁₆"-diameter) red buttons
- 1 package red (⅞"-wide) single-fold bias tape
- Pearl cotton, size 5: white and red
- Embroidery floss: white and red
- Large-eye hand-sewing needle
- Fiberfill stuffing
- Template material
- Fusible web with paper release
- No-fray solution
- Fabric glue (optional)
- Thread
- Basic sewing tools and supplies

PROJECT NOTES
Read all instructions before beginning this project.

Stitch right sides together using a ¼" seam allowance unless otherwise specified.

Materials and cutting lists assume 40" of usable fabric width for yardage.

WOF – width of fabric

HST – half-square triangle ◻

QST – quarter-square triangle ⊠

CUTTING

From red dot cut:
- 10 (6½" x 8½") A rectangles

From red/white stripe cut:
- 5 (2" x 2½") B rectangles

COMPLETING THE PENNANTS

1. Use the pennant bottom curve pattern provided to round off the corners on one end of each A rectangle.

2. Referring to Raw-Edge Fusible Appliqué on page 46, prepare templates for the gingerbread man and cheek shapes using patterns provided. Trace around shapes onto paper side of the fusible web, cut shapes apart and fuse to the wrong side of the appliqué fabrics as listed below. Cut out shapes on drawn lines and remove paper backing.
- Brown tonal: 5 gingerbread men
- Pink dot: 10 cheeks

3. Center a gingerbread man appliqué on the right side of an A rectangle with the head about ⅞" down from the straight top (Figure 1). Referring to the photo, place two cheeks on the gingerbread face. Fuse appliqués in place and machine blanket stitch around the edges using matching thread. Repeat with remaining appliqués and four more A rectangles.

Make 5

Figure 1

4. Referring to the Placement Diagram, cut 10 lengths of rickrack for the arms and another 10 for the legs. Apply no-fray solution to the cut ends and let dry. Tack or glue each piece of rickrack in place.

5. Referring again to the Placement Diagram, sew two ³⁄₁₆"-diameter white buttons to each gingerbread man's face for eyes. Referring to the stitch illustration on page 42, backstitch a smile on each gingerbread man's face.

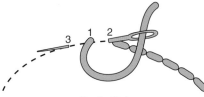

Backstitch

6. Place an appliquéd pennant front and a plain A rectangle together, right sides facing, and pin to a batting rectangle. Sew around the pennant, leaving the top open (Figure 2). Trim the batting close to the seam, clip the curve and turn right side out. Press the edges flat. Repeat with remaining appliquéd pennant fronts and A rectangles.

Figure 2

7. Topstitch ¼" from the seams on the pennants. Quilt by stitching around the gingerbread man or as desired. Stitch across the top inside the ¼" seam allowance to hold.

8. Fold a B rectangle so it measures 2" x 2¼" (Figure 3a). Sew the raw edges together, leaving a 1" opening on the long edge. Trim the corners and turn right side out. Using a doubled length of red thread, sew gathering stitches up the center of the rectangle; pull thread to gather tightly and wrap thread around the center several times to complete one bow tie (Figure 3b). Knot but do not clip the thread. Make five.

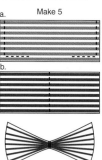

Figure 3

9. Sew a red button to the center front of the bow tie using the attached thread and tack the bow tie to the gingerbread neck to complete the pennant. Make five.

COMPLETING THE ORNAMENTS

1. Prepare templates for the large and small heart using the patterns provided. Use templates to cut out hearts as listed below:
- White felt: 8 large hearts
- Red felt: 4 small hearts

2. Referring to the Placement Diagram, place a red heart in the center of a white heart and hand blanket stitch around the edges using red floss. Make four.

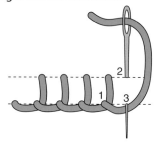

Blanket Stitch

3. Place an appliquéd heart and a plain white heart wrong sides together and blanket stitch around the edges with white floss. Before closing, stuff with fiberfill to desired firmness. Make four.

4. Thread a large-eye needle with a length of red pearl cotton and take a small stitch at the top back of one heart ornament, leaving two thread tails about 3" long each (Figure 4). Tie a knot near the end so the thread loop measures about 2". Trim the thread tails and pull the loop so the knot sits on the back of the heart. Make four.

Figure 4

COMPLETING THE GARLAND

1. Press the bias tape in half lengthwise. Open one end of the bias tape and fold in the raw edge about ⅜". Refold and press.

2. Measure 12" from the prepared end and mark with a pin (Figure 5). Start sewing the edges together and stop about 1" from the pin. Insert a pennant into the folded tape, starting at the pin, and continue sewing across the pennant. Measure and place a pin 6" away. Continue to sew the tape and stop again about 1" before the pin. Insert the second pennant in the same manner and continue until all five pennants have been added. Measure ahead 12" and cut the tape. Finish the end as in step 1 and stitch to the end.

Figure 5

3. Fold each end over about 1½" and sew one ½"-diameter white button through the layers to form two hanging loops (Figure 6).

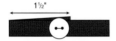

Figure 6

4. Sew a ¾" white button to the tape in the center of each 6" space left between the pennants (Figure 7). These buttons will be for hanging the heart ornaments.

Figure 7

5. Hang the heart ornaments on the buttons between the pennants to complete the garland (Figure 8). ●

Figure 8

Gingerbread Love Garland
Heart Ornament
Placement Diagram 3⅝" x 3¼"

Gingerbread Love Garland
Placement Diagram 6" x 8"

GINGERBREAD LOVE
GARLAND TEMPLATES

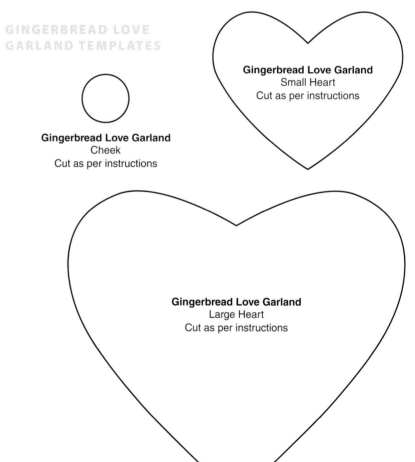

Gingerbread Love Garland
Cheek
Cut as per instructions

Gingerbread Love Garland
Small Heart
Cut as per instructions

Gingerbread Love Garland
Large Heart
Cut as per instructions

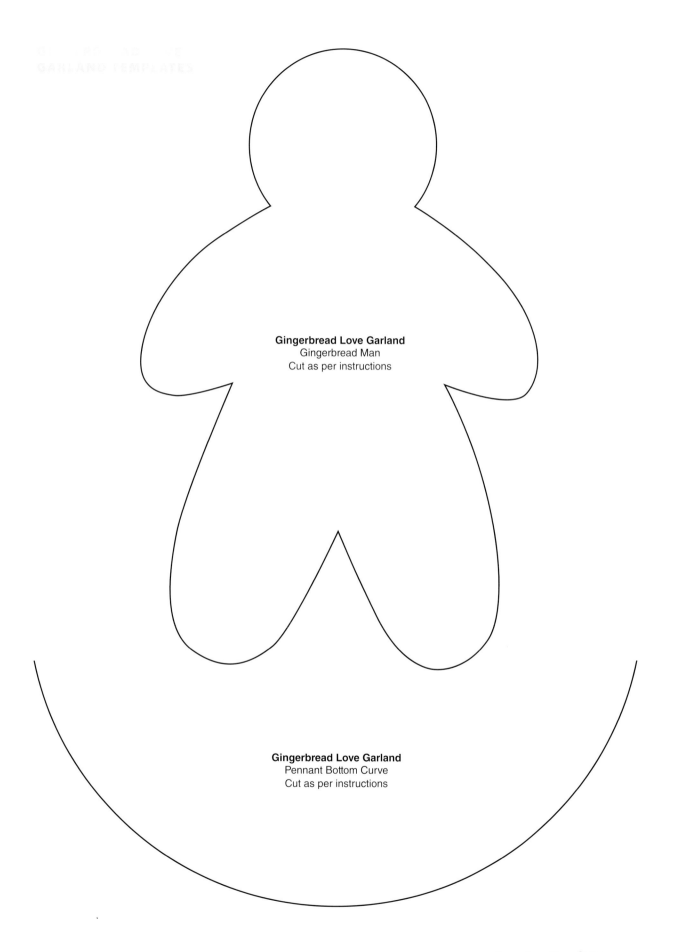

Gingerbread Love Garland
Gingerbread Man
Cut as per instructions

Gingerbread Love Garland
Pennant Bottom Curve
Cut as per instructions

RAW-EDGE FUSIBLE APPLIQUÉ

One of the easiest ways to appliqué is the raw-edge fusible-web method. Individual pieces of paper-backed fusible web are fused to the wrong side of specified fabrics, cut out and then fused together in a motif or individually to a foundation fabric, where they are machine-stitched in place.

Choosing Appliqué Fabrics

Depending on the appliqué, you may want to consider using batiks. Batik is a much tighter weave and, because of the manufacturing process, does not fray. If you are thinking about using regular quilting cottons, be sure to stitch your raw-edge appliqués with blanket/buttonhole stitches instead of a straight stitch.

Cutting Appliqué Pieces

1. Fusible appliqué shapes should be reversed for this technique.

2. Trace the appliqué shapes onto the paper side of paper-backed fusible web. Leave at least ¼" between shapes. Cut out shapes leaving a margin around traced lines. **Note:** *If doing several identical appliqués, trace reversed shapes onto template material to make reusable templates for tracing shapes onto the fusible web.*

3. Follow manufacturer's instructions and fuse shapes to wrong side of fabric as indicated on pattern for color and number to cut.

4. Cut out appliqué shapes on traced lines. Remove paper backing from shapes.

5. Again following fusible web manufacturer's instructions, arrange and fuse pieces to quilt referring to quilt pattern. Or fuse together shapes on top of an appliqué ironing mat to make an appliqué motif that can then be fused to the quilt.

Stitching Appliqué Edges

Machine-stitch appliqué edges to secure the appliqués in place and help finish the raw edges with matching or invisible thread (Photo A). **Note:** *To show stitching, all samples have been stitched with contrasting thread.*

Straight stitch
Photo A

Invisible thread can be used to stitch appliqués down when using the blanket or straight stitches. Do not use it for the satin stitch. Definitely practice with invisible thread before using it on your quilt; it can sometimes be difficult to work with.

A short, narrow buttonhole or blanket stitch is most commonly used (Photo B). Your machine manual may also refer to this as an appliqué stitch. Be sure to stitch next to the appliqué edge with the stitch catching the appliqué.

Buttonhole or blanket stitch
Photo B

Pivot point
Photo C

Practice turning inside and outside corners on scrap fabric before stitching appliqué pieces. Learn how your machine stitches so that you can make the pivot points smooth (Photo C).

1. To stitch outer corners, stitch to the edge of the corner and stop with needle in the fabric at the corner point. Pivot to the next side of the corner and continue to sew (Photo D). You will get a box on an outside corner.

Photo D

2. To stitch inner corners, pivot at the inner point with needle in fabric (Photo E). You will see a Y shape in the corner.

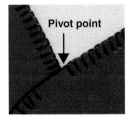
Pivot point
Photo E

3. You can also use a machine straight stitch. Turn corners in the same manner, stitching to the corners and pivoting with needle in down position (Photos F and G).

Photo F

Photo G

General Appliqué Tips

1. Use a light- to medium-weight stabilizer behind an appliqué to keep the fabric from puckering during machine stitching (Photo H).

Photo H

2. To reduce the stiffness of a finished appliqué, cut out the center of the fusible web shape, leaving ¼"–½" inside the pattern line. This gives a border of adhesive to fuse to the background and leaves the center soft and easy to quilt.

3. If an appliqué fabric is so light colored or thin that the background fabric shows through, fuse a lightweight interfacing to the wrong side of the fabric. You can also fuse a piece of the appliqué fabric to a matching piece, wrong sides together, and then apply the fusible web with a drawn pattern to one side. ●

Quilting Basics

The following is a reference guide. For more information, consult a comprehensive quilting book.

Quilt Backing & Batting

Cut your backing and batting 8" larger than the finished quilt-top size and 4" larger for quilts smaller than 50" square. **Note:** *Check with longarm quilter about their requirements, if applicable. For baby quilts not going to a longarm quilter 4"–6" overall may be sufficient.* If preparing the backing from standard-width fabrics, remove the selvages and sew two or three lengths together; press seams open. If using 108"-wide fabric, trim to size on the straight grain of the fabric. Prepare batting the same size as your backing.

Quilting

1. Press quilt top on both sides and trim all loose threads. **Note:** *If you are sending your quilt to a longarm quilter, contact them for specifics about preparing your quilt for quilting.*
2. Mark quilting design on quilt top. Make a quilt sandwich by layering the backing right side down, batting and quilt top centered right side up on flat surface and smooth out. Baste layers together using pins, thread basting or spray basting to hold. **Note:** *Tape or pin backing to surface to hold taut while layering and avoid puckers.*
3. Quilt as desired by hand or machine. Remove pins or basting as you quilt.
4. Trim batting and backing edges even with raw edges of quilt top.

Binding the Quilt

1. Join binding strips on short ends with diagonal seams to make one long strip; trim seams to ¼" and press seams open (Figure 1).

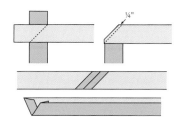

Figure 1

2. Fold ½" of one short end to wrong side and press. Fold the binding strip in half with wrong sides together along length, again referring to Figure 1; press.
3. Starting about 3" from the folded short end, sew binding to quilt top edges, matching raw edges and using a ¼" seam. Stop stitching ¼" from corner and backstitch (Figure 2).

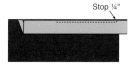

Figure 2

4. Fold binding up at a 45-degree angle to seam and then down even with quilt edges, forming a pleat at corner (Figure 3).

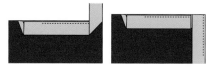

Figure 3

5. Resume stitching from corner edge as shown in Figure 3, down quilt side, backstitching ¼" from next corner. Repeat, mitering all corners, stitching to within 3" of starting point.
6. Trim binding, leaving enough length to tuck inside starting end and complete stitching (Figure 4).

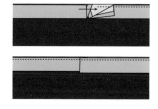

Figure 4

7. If stitching binding by hand, machine-sew binding to the front of the quilt and fold to the back before stitching. If stitching by machine, machine-sew binding to back of the quilt and fold to the front before stitching.

Special Thanks

Please join us in thanking the talented designers
whose work is featured in this collection.

Lyn Brown
Noel Surrounded, 6

Rachelle Craig
Winter Morning, 29

Michelle Freedman
Ribbon Curls Runner, 22

Preeti Harris
Good Tidings, 19

Joy Heimark
Celestial Stars, 25

Chris Malone
Little Tree Basket, 32
Santa Tote, 36
Gingerbread Love Garland, 41

Jill Metzger
Blue Spruce, 15

Wendy Sheppard
Christmas Is Fir Real, 2
Kitties in the Tree, 10

Supplies

We would like to thank the following manufacturers who provided materials
to our designers to make sample projects for this book.

Christmas Is Fir Real, page 2: Fabrics from the Cozy
Wonderland collection by Stephanie Sliwinski of Fancy
That Design House for Moda Fabrics; 50 wt. thread from
Aurifil; Tuscany Silk batting from Hobbs Bonded Fibers.

Noel Surrounded, page 6: Fabrics from Hoffman California-
International Fabrics.

Kitties in the Tree, page 10: Fabrics from the Kitty
Christmas collection by Urban Chiks for Moda Fabrics;
Tuscany Silk batting from Hobbs Bonded Fibers; 50 wt.
thread from Aurifil.

Good Tidings, page 19: Fabric from Island Batik.

Ribbon Curls Runner, page 22: Fabric from the Homemade
Holiday collection by Kris Lammers for Maywood Studio.

Winter Morning, page 29: Fabric from the Cotton Shot
collection by Amanda Murphy for Benartex; Tuscany Wool/
Cotton Blend batting by Hobbs Bonded Fibers.

Santa Tote, page 36: Warm and Natural Cotton Batting from
The Warm Company; 50 wt. Cotton thread from Aurifil.

Annie's® Published by Annie's, 306 East Parr Road, Berne, IN 46711. Printed in USA. Copyright © 2024 Annie's. All rights reserved. This publication may
not be reproduced in part or in whole without written permission from the publisher.

RETAIL STORES: If you would like to carry this publication or any other Annie's publication, visit AnniesWSL.com.

Every effort has been made to ensure that the instructions in this publication are complete and accurate. We cannot, however, take responsibility for human error,
typographical mistakes or variations in individual work. Please visit AnniesCustomerService.com to check for pattern updates.

ISBN: 979-8-89253-360-7
2 3 4 5 6 7 8 9